NOW WHAT?

A MATH TALE

NOW WHAT?

A MATH TALE

Robie H. Harris   illustrated by Chris Chatterton

CANDLEWICK PRESS

WOW!

Blocks. Lots and lots of blocks!

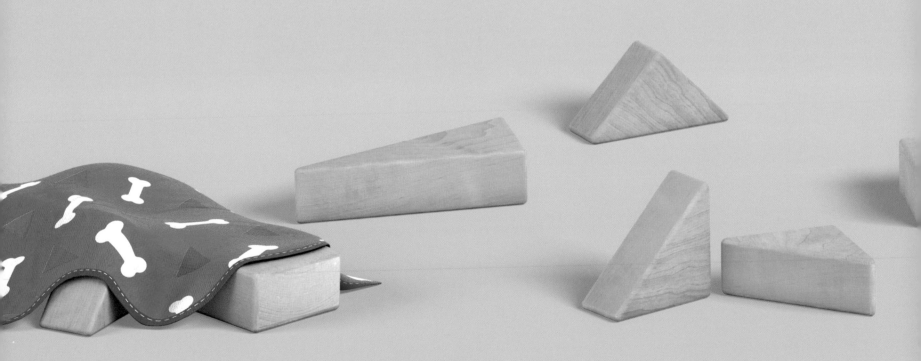

Hey, Bear.

This one's long.

Long enough for a snooze?

Wide enough?

Look! 1. 2. 3. 4 corners.

1. 2. 3. 4 straight lines.

2 are long. 2 are short.

Hey. This is a rectangle!

A rectangle on top.

And a rectangle on the bottom.

Upside down. Down side up.

It's still a rectangle!

Surprise! Every side's a rectangle.

Hey! It's a rectangle block.

Oops.

Too short for a snooze!

Too short for me.

Too skinny.

Okay.

I need 1 more long one.

Just like this one.

Oh no.

There is only 1 rectangle block.

Yikes!

Well . . .

Maybe . . .

This one?

Look! 1. 2. 3. 4 corners.

1. 2. 3. 4 straight lines—all the same size.

Hey. This is a square!

Whoa! A rectangle has 1. 2. 3. 4 straight lines.

And 1. 2. 3. 4 corners.

Oh. This is a rectangle that's square!

And there's a square on top.

And a square on the bottom.

Upside down. Down side up.

It's still a square!

And it's still a rectangle that's square.

Surprise!

Every side is a rectangle!

So, it's a rectangle block—

that's a square block, too!

What if?

Nope. Still too short.

Way too short
for a snooze.

1 more?

1 more square block?

Yep. Long enough.

Nope. Too skinny.
Not wide enough.
Too skinny for me.

I need more square blocks!
Now!

OH-HHH NO-OOO!

No more rectangle blocks?

No more square blocks?

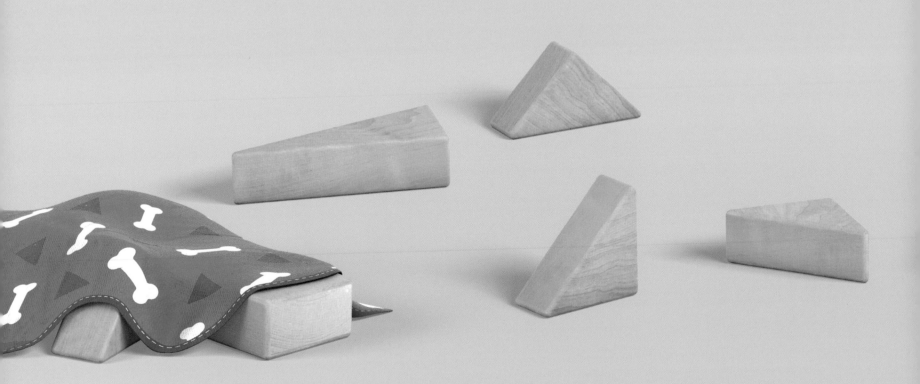

NOW WHAT?

Oh. More blocks.

With 1. 2. 3 corners.

1. 2. 3 straight lines.

Hey. They're triangle blocks!

Look.
Triangle on top.
Triangle on the bottom.
Upside down. Down side up.

Surprise! It's still a triangle!

Okay.

1 big triangle block.

Right here.

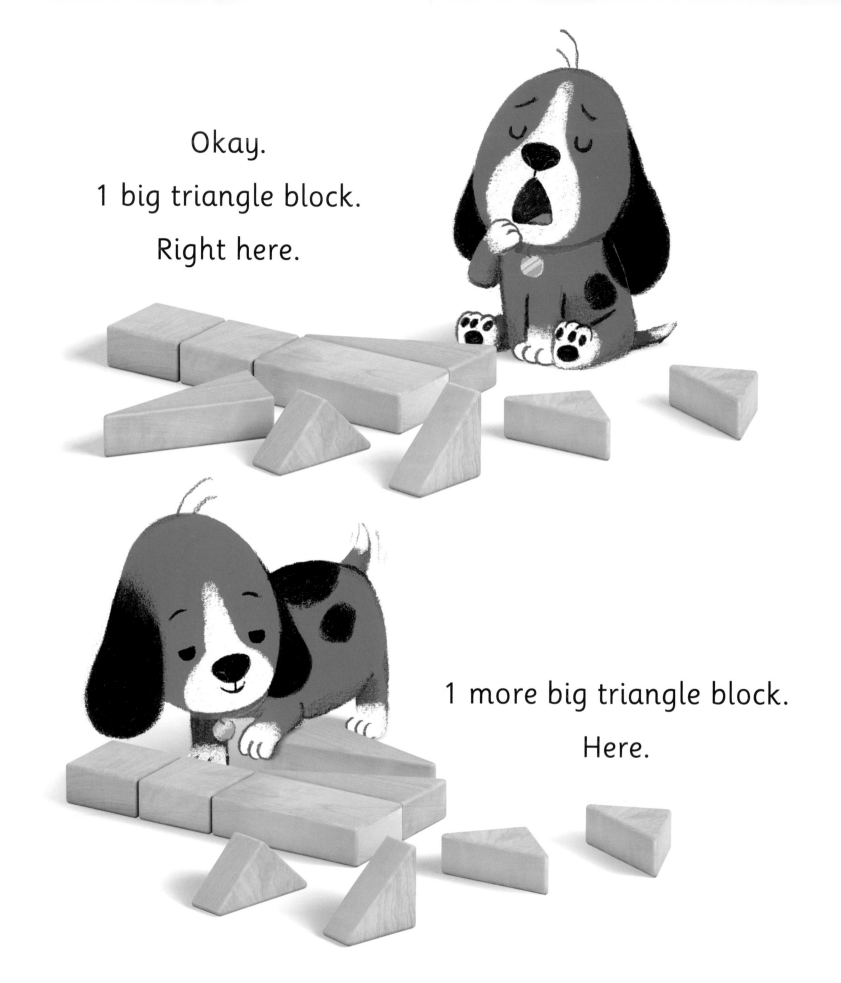

1 more big triangle block.

Here.

1 small triangle block.
And 1 more small triangle block.
Here.

1 more small triangle block.
And . . . 1 more!
Right here.

Long enough for me!

Now it's wide enough.

Hey! I made a bed.

Surprise! It's a rectangle bed.

OH?

2 more blocks.

1 more rectangle block.

1 more triangle block.

DONE!

I'm so-ooo tired now.

So-ooo very tired.

DOG TIRED!

Okay, Bear.

Snooze time!

zzzzzzZZZ...

For "Block Builders" Rosie, Daisy, Ella, Sam, David, and Ben for inspiring me to write this book. For Hal Melnick and David Harris, who shared their deep understanding of math and young children along with their expertise, insights, and criticism when responding to my nonstop queries. For Ellen Kelley, Emily Linsay, Bill Harris, Robyn Heilbrun, and Elizabeth Levy for being there for all my on-the-spot questions.

R. H. H.

Thank you to everyone at Community Playthings for the beautiful wooden blocks you make with the utmost care and precision—blocks that allow children of all ages to wonder, explore, play, think, create, even fail, and finally to feel the pride of success, all while discovering endless math and science concepts.

Text copyright © 2019 by Robie H. Harris. Illustrations copyright © 2019 by Chris Chatterton. All rights reserved. No part of this book may be reproduced, transmitted, or stored in an information retrieval system in any form or by any means, graphic, electronic, or mechanical, including photocopying, taping, and recording, without prior written permission from the publisher. First edition 2019. Library of Congress Catalog Card Number pending. ISBN 978-0-7636-7828-9. This book was typeset in Sassoon Primary. The illustrations were done in pencil and colored digitally. Candlewick Press, 99 Dover Street, Somerville, Massachusetts 02144. visit us at www.candlewick.com.
Printed in Shenzhen, Guangdong, China. 19 20 21 22 23 24 CCP 10 9 8 7 6 5 4 3 2 1

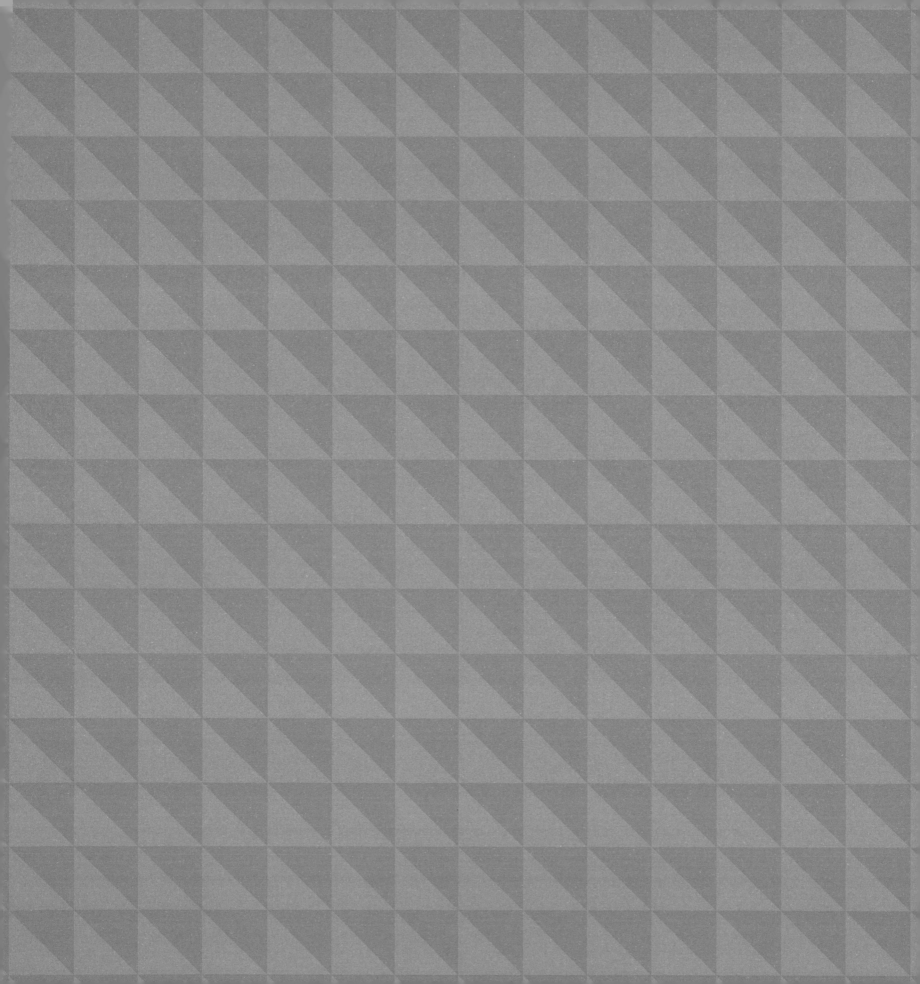